BAKING

TIGER BOOKS INTERNATIONAL
LONDON

Introduction

Baking is a particularly satisfying branch of cookery and one which weaves a special kind of spell over cooks of all ages. Creating your own breads, cakes and biscuits is a joy many have learned from their mothers and grandmothers who have passed recipes and tips down through the generations. This has its advantages, but also means many people often stick only to these tried and tested recipes and forget the wealth of exciting and unusual ideas which are both simple and delicious.

Many people who have little cooking experience mistakenly believe that baking is difficult. This is just not true. There is no great mystery in producing good baking, the trick is to start off with something simple and progress from there. In many ways we are very lucky today, as modern technology provides us with a range of time-saving appliances such as food processors, mixers and freezers. So now, as well as mixing our bread quickly, we can make four loaves at a time and freeze them.

The techniques used in baking are generally straightforward and one of the great advantages of baking is that many ingredients can be altered, removed or added to. Flour is a particularly good example of this – most recipes using white flour can be replaced with brown flour or a mixture of half brown and half white, whichever suits your taste. Biscuits, always a great source of fun for kids, can be adapted by adding chocolate or fruit, for instance. Half the enjoyment of baking is experimenting and it is this process of altering and finc-tuning recipes which ensures that baking remains a fascinating pastime for many cooks.

This book contains a delicious mixture of recipes ranging from scones to teabreads, cakes to biscuits and breads, all tried and tested. And with an easy-to-follow format and a colour photograph of each finished recipe, you will discover that producing the perfect result is simpler than you ever imagined.

3290
This edition published in 1993 by Tiger Books International PLC, London
© 1993 Coombe Books
Printed and bound in Singapore
ISBN 1 85501 308 8

YOGURT SCONES

Serve with jam and cream.

MAKES 10 SCONES

50g/2oz vegetable margarine or butter
225g/8oz wholemeal self-raising flour
25g/1oz demerara sugar
25g/1oz raisins
Plain yogurt to mix

---

1. Rub the fat into the flour and sugar.

2. Add the raisins and mix well.

3. Add enough yogurt to mix to a fairly stiff dough.

4. Turn the mixture out onto a floured board and knead lightly. Make two large circles of dough or cut into 2 inch rounds.

5. Bake in hot oven for 15-17 minutes at 210°C/425°F/Gas Mark 7.

6. Remove and cool on a wire rack.

TIME: Preparation takes 10 minutes, cooking takes 15-17 minutes.

VARIATION: Use chopped dried apricots instead of raisins.

OATLET COOKIES

A delicious mix of oats, seeds and syrup
makes these cookies extra special.

MAKES 10 COOKIES

100g/4oz porridge oats
100g/4oz plain flour
90g/3oz sunflower seeds
25g/1oz sesame seeds
½ tsp mixed spice
100g/4oz margarine
1 tbsp brown sugar
1 tsp golden syrup or molasses
½ tsp bread soda
1 tbsp boiling water
225g/8oz carob drops

1. Mix the oats, flour, sunflower seeds, sesame seeds and spice together.

2. Melt the margarine, sugar and golden syrup or molasses over a gentle heat.

3. Add the bread soda and water to the syrup mixture and stir well.

4. Pour over dry ingredients and mix.

5. Place spoonfuls of the mixture well apart onto a greased baking tray and bake for 10 minutes at 190°C/375°F/Gas Mark 5.

6. Allow to cool on the tray.

7. Melt the carob drops in a bowl over hot water and place teaspoonsful of the melted carob on top of the cookies. Leave to set. Store in an airtight tin.

TIME: Preparation takes 15 minutes, cooking takes 10 minutes.

VARIATION: Ground ginger can be used in place of the mixed spice.

COOK'S TIP: A block of carob may be used in place of the carob drops.

ALMOND LAYER GATEAU

Definitely not for the diet conscious, but delicious for those wishing to sin. This wonderful creamy gateau is ideal for serving with tea, or even as a dessert.

MAKES ONE 20CM/8-INCH ROUND CAKE

60g/2oz dried white breadcrumbs
100ml/4fl oz milk
2 tbsps rum
90g/3oz unsalted butter or margarine
90g/3oz caster sugar
6 eggs, separated
90g/3oz ground roasted almonds
570ml/1 pint double cream
2 tbsps icing sugar
60g/2oz roasted almonds, finely chopped
Whole blanched almonds, lightly toasted
   for decoration

1. Put the breadcrumbs into a large bowl and pour over the milk and 1 tbsp of the rum. Allow to stand for 15 minutes or until the liquid has been completely absorbed.

2. Put the butter in a large bowl and beat until soft. Gradually add the sugar and continue mixing until it is light and fluffy.

3. Beat the egg yolks, one at a time, into the butter mixture. Stir well to prevent it curdling.

4. Add the soaked breadcrumbs to the egg and butter mixture, folding them well to blend evenly.

5. Whisk the egg whites until they are stiff, but not dry. Fold these into the egg and butter mixture, along with the ground almonds.

6. Lightly grease three 20cm/8-inch round cake tins, and dust each one lightly with a little flour. Line the base of each tin with silicone paper or lightly greased greaseproof paper.

7. Divide the cake mixture equally between the three tins. Bake in a preheated oven 180°C/350°F/Gas Mark 4, for 30-35 minutes, until well risen and golden brown.

8. Allow the cakes to cool briefly in the tins before gently loosening the sides and turning onto a wire rack to cool completely.

9. Whip the cream until it is stiff, then beat in the icing sugar and remaining rum.

10. Reserve one third of the cream in a separate bowl, and fold the finely chopped almonds into the remaining two-thirds.

11. Sandwich the cake layers together with the almond cream, then spread the plain cream onto the top, reserving some for piping.

12. Fit a piping bag with a small rosette nozzle and pipe rosettes of cream onto the top of the cake. Decorate with the toasted whole almonds and serve.

TIME: Prepartion takes 40 minutes, cooking takes 35 minutes.

COOK'S TIP: Refrigerate the cream for at least 2 hours before whipping, to obtain better results.

SHORTBREAD BISCUITS

*Sandwich these biscuits together with raspberry
jam for children's birthday parties.*

MAKES ABOUT 18

150g/5oz unbleached white flour
37g/2½ oz light muscovado sugar, finely
   ground
100g/4oz soft margarine
½ tsp vanilla essence

1. Sieve the flour and sugar together and rub in the margarine.

2. Add the vanilla essence and bind the mixture together.

3. Form into small balls and place on a baking tray a few inches apart.

4. With the back of a fork, press the balls down making a criss-cross pattern.

5. Bake at 190°C/375°F/Gas Mark 4 for about 10-15 minutes until golden brown in colour.

6. Cool and store in an airtight container.

TIME: Preparation takes 10 minutes, cooking takes 10-15 minutes.

VARIATIONS: Add a tablespoon of currants to make fruit biscuits.
Omit the vanilla essence and substitute almond essence to make almond biscuits.

SCOFA BREAD

*The ideal chunky bread to serve warm with
a ploughman's lunch or lunchtime salad meals.*

MAKES 1 LOAF

550g/1¼ lbs self-raising wholemeal flour
225g/8oz bran
1 tsp salt
100g/4oz vegetable fat
Just under 570ml/1 pint water
1 tbsp vegetable oil

1. Put the flour, bran and salt into a
mixing bowl.

2. Rub in the fat and mix the water and oil
together.

3. Make a well in the centre of the flour
and pour in the water and oil.

4. Mix in the flour, drawing it into the
liquid mixture gradually from the sides,
until a dough is formed.

5. Shape into a 17.8cm/7 inch round and
place on a greased baking tray.

6. With a sharp knife cut to within ½ inch
of the bottom making four sections.

7. Bake just above the centre of the oven,
200°C/400°F/Gas Mark 6 for about 1 hour
or until nicely browned and 'hollow'
sounding when tapped with the back of
your fingers.

8. Remove from the oven and wrap in a
clean tea towel to cool.

TIME: Preparation takes 10 minutes, cooking takes 1 hour.

COOK'S TIP: Eat within a couple of days.

CARROT CAKE

Carrots give a cake a delicious sweet flavour, as well as lots of vitamins and minerals. What better excuse do you need to indulge in this delicious tea-time treat.

MAKES 1 X 25CM/10-INCH LOAF

175g/6oz butter
175g/6oz soft brown sugar
2 eggs, well beaten
225g/8oz plain wholemeal flour
1½ tsps bicarbonate of soda
½ tsp baking powder
¼ tsp ground cinnamon
¼ tsp ground nutmeg
½ tsp salt
225g/8oz peeled carrots, grated
90g/3oz raisins
60g/2oz finely chopped walnuts
¼ tsp cardamom seeds, crushed
Icing sugar, for dredging

1. Cream the butter and sugar together until they are light and fluffy.

2. Add the eggs a little at a time, beating well and adding a teaspoonful of the flour with each addition, to prevent the mixture from curdling.

3. Put the remaining flour into a large bowl along with the bicarbonate of soda, baking powder, cinnamon, nutmeg and salt. Mix together well.

4. Carefully fold the flour into the butter and egg mixture, mixing well to ensure that it is blended evenly.

5. Add the carrots, raisins, nuts and cardamom seeds, beating the mixture well to blend evenly.

6. Lightly grease a 25cm/10 inch loaf tin and line the base with a piece of silicone paper.

7. Pour the cake mixture into the loaf tin, and bake in a preheated oven 180°C/ 350°F/Gas Mark 4, for 45-50 minutes or until a fine metal skewer comes out clean when inserted into the centre of the cake.

8. Cool the cake in its tin for 15 minutes before turning out onto a wire rack to cool completely.

9. Dredge the cake with icing sugar just before serving.

TIME: Preparation takes 30 minutes, cooking takes 45-50 minutes.

WATCHPOINT: If the egg and butter mixture should curdle, add a little more flour and beat very hard with an electric whis.

GINGER SNAPS

A great favourite for tea breaks.

MAKES 18-20

100g/4oz plain wholemeal flour
1½ level tsps baking powder
1½ level tsps ground ginger
50g/2oz soft brown sugar
Rind and juice of ½ lemon
3 tbsps golden syrup
50g/2oz margarine

1. Sift the flour, baking powder, ginger and sugar into a mixing bowl.

2. Add the lemon rind and juice.

3. Melt the syrup and margarine over a low heat and stir into the dry ingredients.

4. Leave to cool.

5. Roll into small balls and place well apart on greased baking trays.

6. Flatten out slightly with the back of a fork, still keeping their shape.

7. Cook at 190°C/375°F/Gas Mark 5 for 10-15 minutes.

8. Allow to cool for 2 minutes and then remove to a wire rack.

TIME: Preparation takes 10 minutes, cooking takes 10-15 minutes.

VARIATION: Substitute cinnamon for the ginger and sprinkle with chopped nuts.

COOK'S TIP: As the biscuits cool they will become crisp. Store in an airtight tin.

CRUNCH

*If kept for a couple of days the Crunch will
become deliciously soft and sticky.*

MAKES 24 SQUARES

225g/8oz butter or margarine
2 tbsps golden syrup
450g/1lb oats
225g/8oz soft brown sugar

---

1. Put the butter and syrup into a pan and melt gently over a low heat.

2. Place the oats in a large mixing bowl and mix in the sugar.

3. Pour the melted butter and syrup over the oats and mix well with a wooden spoon.

4. Put the mixture into a 30.5 x 20.3cm/12 x 8 inch Swiss roll tin and flatten well with the back of a spoon.

5. Bake in the centre of a 180°C/350°F/ Gas Mark 4 oven for 30-35 minutes until golden brown on top.

6. Remove from the oven, allow to cool for 2-3 minutes and mark into squares.

7. Leave until nearly cold before removing.

8. Store in an airtight tin.

TIME: Preparation takes 10 minutes, cooking takes 30-35 minutes.

VARIATION: Use half oats and half unsweetened muesli.

CAROB BISCUIT CAKE

A very rich and delicious cake.

MAKES 16 SQUARES

225g/8oz digestive biscuits
100g/4oz margarine or butter
1 tbsp brown sugar
3 level tbsps carob powder
2 tbsps golden syrup
150g/5oz sultanas
225g/8oz carob bar

1. Crush the biscuits with a rolling pin and place in a mixing bowl.

2. Put the margarine, sugar, carob powder and syrup into a pan and melt over a low heat, stirring all the time.

3. Add to the biscuit crumbs together with the sultanas.

4. Mix very thoroughly.

5. Press the mixture into a 20.3cm/8-inch square container.

6. Break the carob bar into a heatproof bowl and place over a pan of simmering water until melted.

7. Cover the cake with the melted carob and mark it with the back of a fork.

8. Refrigerate until cold.

9. Cut into squares and store in an airtight tin.

TIME: Preparation takes 20-25 minutes plus chilling time.

BANANA LOAF

*Eat on its own as a cake, or slice thinly and
butter to serve for elevenses or afternoon tea.*

MAKES 1 LOAF

1 tea cup of porridge oats
1 tea cup of sugar
1 tea cup of mixed fruit
1 tea cup of Granose banana soya milk
1 large cup of self-raising flour
Pinch of nutmeg

1. Begin preparing the cake the day before it is to be cooked. Place all the ingredients except the self-raising flour and nutmeg into a large bowl and stir well.

2. Cover and put into the refrigerator overnight.

3. The following day, line or grease a 1lb loaf tin.

4. Mix the self-raising flour and the nutmeg gently into the mixture and put into the loaf tin.

5. Bake at 180°C/350°F/Gas Mark 4 for an hour or until a skewer inserted into the loaf comes out clean.

TIME: Preparation takes 10 minutes, cooking takes 1 hour.

VARIATIONS: ½ a tsp of mixed spice may be used in place of the nutmeg. Ordinary milk or plain soya milk can be used instead of banana soya milk.

COOK'S TIP: The loaf becomes more moist if left in an airtight tin for a day or two before eating.

RICH FRUIT CAKE WITH GUINNESS

A deliciously moist fruit cake which is easy to make.

MAKES 1 CAKE

225g/8oz soft margarine
225g/8oz dark brown sugar
4 medium eggs
275g/10oz wholemeal flour
1 dstsp mixed spice
500g/1lb 2oz mixed dried fruit
10 tbsps Guinness

1. Cream the margarine and sugar together.

2. Beat in the eggs one at a time.

3. Gradually stir in the flour and mixed spice.

4. Mix in the dried fruit.

5. Add 4 tbsps Guinness to mix.

6. Place the mixture into a 17.8cm/7 inch loose-bottomed cake tin and make a deep well in the centre, this allows the finished cake to have a flat top.

7. Cook for 1 hour at 170°C/325°F/Gas Mark 3 and then turn down to 150°C/300°F/Gas Mark 2 for a further 1½ hours.

8. Allow the cake to cool in the tin.

9. Remove and turn upside down. Prick the base of the cake all over with a skewer and slowly pour over the remaining 6 tbsps of Guinness.

10. Store in a cool place for at least a week before eating.

TIME: Preparation takes about 15 minutes, cooking takes 2½ hours.

SERVING IDEA: Use for birthdays and special occasions or serve with chunks of mature cheese.

VARIATION: This mixture can be cooked in two 1lb loaf tins, reduce the final cooking time and cook until a skewer inserted into the cake comes out clean.

Wholewheat Brown Bread

This is a very moist bread which will last for days.

MAKES 2 LOAVES

750g/1½ lbs wholewheat flour
1 tea cup white flour
1 tea cup porridge oats
1 tea cup bran
1 tea cup pinhead oatmeal
½ tea cup wheatgerm
½ tsp bicarbonate of soda
½ tsp sea salt
1.2 ltrs/2 pints milk
2 eggs, beaten

1. Heat the oven to 180°C/350°F/ Gas Mark 4.

2. Mix all the dry ingredients together.

3. Mix the milk and eggs and add to the dry ingredients.

4. Spoon into 2 greased 1lb loaf tins and bake in the centre of the oven for 1¼ to 1½ hours.

5. Turn out to cool on a wire rack.

TIME: Preparation takes about 20 minutes, cooking takes 1¼ to 1½ hours.

VARIATION: A handful of caraway seeds can be added to the mixture and some sprinkled on the top before baking.

GRIDDLE SCONES

*The whole fun of these cakes is that they can be eaten
directly from the pan in which they are cooked. So gather family
and friends around you for a traditional tea-time treat.*

SERVES 4-6

100g/4oz self-raising flour
Pinch salt
45g/1½ oz butter or margarine
100g/4oz currants
½ tsp ground nutmeg
1 egg
90ml/3fl oz milk

---

1. Mix the flour and salt together, and rub in the butter until the mixture resembles fine breadcrumbs.

2. Stir in the currants and the nutmeg, then push the mixture gently to the sides of the bowl to form a well in the centre.

3. Beat together the egg and the milk, and pour into the well in the centre of the flour.

4. Using a wooden spoon, mix the egg and milk mixture into the flour, stirring from the centre of the bowl and drawing the flour in from the sides to form a smooth, thick batter.

5. Heat a heavy-based frying pan on top of a moderate heat, and grease with a little butter or oil.

6. Drop tablespoons of the batter into the hot pan, and cook for 2-3 minutes, or until the bases are set and have turned golden brown.

7. Turn the scones over and cook on the other side in the same way.

8. Serve from the pan with preserves.

TIME: Preparation takes 15 minutes, cooking takes about 4 minutes per scone.

PREPARTION: If the batter is too thick, add a little extra milk until it becomes a soft dropping consistency.

FREEZING: These scones freeze well, and can be re-heated by wrapping in a clean tea towel and standing in a warm oven until they are heated through.

PRUNE AND WALNUT LOAF

If you do not have prunes, dates taste just as good.

MAKES 1 LOAF

350g/12oz prunes
175ml/6fl.oz water
350g/12oz fine wholemeal flour
2 tsps baking powder
50g/2oz brown sugar
1 tsp mixed spice
100g/4oz walnuts, chopped
4 tbsps sunflower oil
1 egg
Orange juice
Whole walnuts to decorate

1. Simmer the prunes in the water until soft. Allow to cool.

2. Retain the cooking liquid, remove the stones and chop the prunes finely.

3. Mix the flour, baking powder, sugar, spice and walnuts together.

4. In a separate bowl mix the prunes, cooking liquid, oil and egg.

5. Fold together the flour mixture and the prune mixture, adding orange juice to give a soft consistency.

6. Put into a greased and lined 900g/2lb loaf tin.

7. Decorate with walnuts.

8. Bake at 170°C/325°F/Gas Mark 3 for 1¼ hours.

TIME: Preparation takes 15 minutes, cooking takes 1¼ hours.

FREEZING: Freeze after cooking for up to 2 months.

FRUIT SCONES

*Scones are always a firm favourite and do not need
any added sugar when made with plenty of fruit.*

SERVES 10-12

225g/8oz plain flour
1 tsp cream of tartar
½ tsp bicarbonate of soda
¼ tsp salt
45g/1½ oz butter
75g/3oz sultanas
15g/½ oz sunflower seeds
15g/½ oz fresh stem ginger
2 eggs
Extra milk for blending
Beaten egg, for glaze

1. Mix the flour, cream of tartar, bicarbonate of soda and salt together, and sieve it twice through a metal sieve to aerate completely.

2. Put the sieved flour into a large bowl, and rub in the butter until the mixture resembles fine breadcrumbs.

3. Stir the sultanas and the sunflower seeds into the flour and butter mixture.

4. Peel the ginger, and cut or grate it into very small pieces.

5. Using a pestle and mortar or the handle of a large knife, crush the ginger until it becomes a paste.

6. Put the ginger into a small bowl along with the eggs, and beat together with a fork until they are evenly blended.

7. Add the beaten eggs and ginger to the flour and sultana mixture, mixing well to form a soft dough, and adding a little extra milk if the dough is too stiff.

8. Lightly flour a work surface. Turn out the dough and knead it lightly until it becomes smooth.

9. Roll the dough out to approximately 1.25cm/½-inch thick.

10. Cut the dough into 5cm/2-inch rounds using a biscuit cutter.

11. Place the scones on a greased baking sheet, and brush each one with the extra beaten egg. Bake in a preheated oven 200°C/400°F/Gas Mark 6 for 10-15 minutes, or until golden brown and well risen.

TIME: Preparation takes approximately 15 minutes, cooking takes 10-15 minutes.

PREPARATION: Do not roll the dough out too thinly, otherwise the scones will not rise properly.

VARIATION: Use other combinations of dried fruit and nuts, or seeds, in place of the sultanas and sunflower seeds in this recipe.

FRUIT CAKE

This cake freezes well.

MAKES 1 CAKE

350g/12oz plain wholemeal flour
1 tsp mixed spice
1½ tsps bicarbonate of soda
175g/6oz margarine
175g/6oz demerara sugar
175g/6oz currants
75g/3oz sultanas
280ml/½ pint soya milk
1 tbsp lemon juice

1. Sift the flour, spice and bicarbonate of soda together into a large bowl.

2. Rub in the fat until the mixture resembles fine breadcrumbs.

3. Add the sugar, currants and sultanas.

4. Mix the milk and lemon juice together and add to the dry ingredients.

5. Mix well to form a dropping consistency.

6. Leave the mixture overnight.

7. Turn into a prepared 25cm x 12cm/10 x 5 inch tin.

8. Bake in the centre of the oven at 160°C/325°F/Gas Mark 3 for 2 hours.

TIME: Preparation takes 20 minutes, cooking takes 2 hours.

VARIATION: Use sour milk in place of the milk/lemon mixture.

CHOC-OAT SLICES

Perfect for the lunch box or a kiddies party.

MAKES 12 SLICES

100g/4oz carob bar
100g/4oz hard margarine
1 tbsp clear honey
225g/8oz porridge oats
100g/4oz sultanas
50g/2oz dessicated coconut

1. Break the carob into a pan and add the margarine and honey.

2. Melt over a very low heat and stir until all the ingredients have melted.

3. Remove from the heat and add the oats, sultanas and coconut.

4. Spread the mixture evenly into a greased rectangular baking tin and bake at 180°C/350°F/Gas Mark 4 for 25-30 minutes.

5. Cool slightly and cut into slices.

6. When completely cold, remove and store in an airtight tin.

TIME: Preparation takes 10 minutes, cooking takes 25-30 minutes.

VARIATION: Raisins may be used in place of the sultanas.
Try maple syrup instead of honey.

SULTANA SODA BREAD

*Sultanas add a natural sweetness which makes this
bread ideal for serving as a tea-time treat.*

SERVES 6-8

450g/1lb plain white flour
1 tsp salt
1 tsp bicarbonate of soda
1 tsp cream of tartar
80ml/½ pint sour milk
100g/4oz sultanas

---

1. Sift together the flour, salt, bicarbonate of soda and cream of tartar in a mixing bowl.

2. Add the sultanas and mix into the flour quickly, making a slight well in the centre of the flour as you do so.

3. Pour the milk into the well in the flour, and mix with a round bladed knife to form a firm, but not too stiff dough.

4. Turn the dough onto a lightly floured board, and knead quickly to bring all the ingredients together well.

5. Shape the dough into a round, and flatten it slightly with the palm of your hand.

6. Place the dough round on a lightly greased and floured baking sheet. Cut a deep cross into the top of the dough with a sharp knife.

7. Bake the dough in a preheated oven 200°C/400°F/Gas Mark 6 for 25 minutes.

8. After this time, turn the loaf upside down on the tray and return to the oven for a further 10 minutes to dry out completely.

9. Wrap the baked loaf in a damp cloth, and place on a wire rack to cool completely.

TIME: Preparation takes 15 minutes, cooking takes 35 minutes.

VARIATION: Use wholemeal flour instead of the white flour in this recipe.

PREPARATION: To test that the loaf is completely cooked, tap the base with your fingers and if it sounds hollow it is ready.

COOK'S TIP: If you do not have sour milk, use fresh milk with 1 tbsp of natural yogurt added.

OATMEAL AND TREACLE SCONES

A tasty alternative to plain scones.

MAKES ABOUT 12 SCONES

100g/4oz plain wholemeal flour
2 level tsps baking powder
Pinch of salt
25g/1oz margarine
100g/4oz oatmeal
1 tbsp molasses
Milk to bind

1. Sieve the flour, baking powder and salt into a bowl three times.

2. Rub in the margarine, then add the oatmeal.

3. Warm the molasses and 1 tbsp of the milk.

4. Bind the flour mixture with the molasses and milk, adding extra milk as necessary.

5. Roll out to ¼ inch thick and cut into 2 inch circles.

6. Bake on a greased baking sheet at 220°C/425°F/Gas Mark 7 for 10 minutes.

7. Remove and place on a wire rack to cool.

TIME: Preparation takes 10 minutes, cooking takes 10 minutes.

FREEZING: The scones may be placed in a freezer bag or container and frozen after cooking.

GINGERBREAD

Dark treacle and fresh ginger combine to
make this favourite family cake.

MAKES ONE 17.5CM/7-INCH SQUARE CAKE

100g/4oz unsalted butter
100ml/4fl oz black treacle
225g/8oz light soft brown sugar
100ml/4fl oz hot water
300g/10oz plain flour
2 tsps baking powder
2 tsps grated fresh ginger, peeled
1 tsp grated nutmeg
1 egg, beaten

1. Put the butter into a large saucepan, along with the treacle and sugar. Heat gently, stirring all the time, until the sugar and butter have melted together.

2. Pour in the hot water, mix well and set aside.

3. Sift the flour with the baking powder into a large bowl. Make a well in the centre, and add the ginger, nutmeg and beaten egg.

4. Gradually beat in the treacle and butter, using a wooden spoon and carefully drawing the flour from the outside into the centre.

5. Line the base of the cake tin with silicone or lightly oiled greaseproof paper.

6. Pour the gingerbread mixture into the cake tin, and bake in a preheated oven 160°C/325°F/Gas Mark 3, for 1-1½ hours, testing during this time with a skewer; which should come out clean when the cake is cooked.

7. Allow the cake to cool in the tin, before turning out onto a wire rack.

TIME: Preparation takes about 15 minutes, cooking takes 1-1½ hours.

VARIATION: Add 60g/2oz chopped mixed fruit to the gingerbread mixture along with the spices.

SERVING IDEA: Serve as a dessert with a lemon sauce.

SAFFRON TEACAKES

*The use of sweet spices in baking will reduce
the necessity to add salt to recipes.*

MAKES 10-12 TEACAKES

140ml/¼ pint milk
Good pinch saffron
225g/8oz self-raising flour
100g/4oz unsalted butter
100g/4oz currants
½ tsp allspice
25g/1oz candied peel
50g/2oz caster sugar
1 egg, beaten

1. Heat 60ml/4 tbsps of the milk in a small saucepan and add the saffron. Allow to stand for 10-15 minutes to infuse.

2. Sift the flour into a large bowl and cut the butter into this with a knife, until it is reduced to very small pieces.

3. Stir the currants, allspice, peel and sugar into the flour and butter mixture.

4. Make a well in the centre of the flour and stir in the saffron milk and the remainder of the milk. Mix well to form a soft dough.

5. Turn the dough onto a lightly floured board, and knead until smooth.

6. Roll the dough into a circle approximately ½ -inch thick. Cut into 10-12 rounds with a 7.5cm/3-inch pastry cutter.

7. Arrange the individual rounds on a lightly greased baking sheet, and brush the top with a little beaten egg.

8. Bake the cakes in a preheated oven, 180°C/350°F/Gas Mark 4, for 20-30 minutes, until they are well risen and golden brown.

TIME: Preparation takes 15 minutes, cooking takes 20-30 minutes.

COOK'S TIP: Do not be tempted to use too much saffron; a little will go a very long way.

SOFT BREAD CAKES

The bread cakes may be split and toasted, buttered and then filled with sizzling cheese or fried eggs to make a nutritious and satisfying snack meal.

MAKES 6

350g/12oz wholewheat flour
1 tsp salt
25g/1oz fresh yeast
1 tsp brown sugar
1 tea cup of milk
25g/1oz vegetable fat
1 egg, beaten

1. Put the flour and salt in a mixing bowl.

2. Cream the yeast and sugar together until liquid.

3. Warm the milk with the vegetable fat.

4. Mix the milk and fat with the creamed yeast and stir in the beaten egg.

5. Make a hollow in the flour and work the milk mixture in gradually to make a soft dough.

6. Knead a little and form into six round cakes.

7. Cover and leave to rise for 20 minutes in a warm place.

8. Bake 220°C/425°F/Gas Mark 7 for about 15 minutes.

9. Glaze with beaten egg or milk and sugar a few minutes before removing from the oven.

TIME: Preparation takes 30 minutes, cooking takes 15 minutes.

VARIATION: Make Currant Tea Cakes by adding 75g/3oz currants and 50g/2oz sugar to the recipe in the mixing.

APRICOT AND WALNUT TEABREAD

*Good news for those with a sweet tooth, cakes and teabreads
are an excellent and delicious way of introducing fibre
into the diet, and this recipe is no exception.*

MAKES 1 LOAF

175g/6oz polyunsaturated margarine
100g/4oz unrefined soft brown sugar,
   or molasses
3 eggs, beaten
225g/8oz wholemeal self-raising flour
2 tbsps skimmed milk
100g/4oz dried apricots, chopped
60g/2oz shelled walnuts, chopped
2 tsps clear honey, warmed
Few extra chopped dried apricots, to
   decorate

1. Lightly grease a 1kg/2lb loaf tin and
line the base with a piece of greaseproof
paper.

2. Cream together the margarine and
sugar, until light and fluffy.

3. Beat in the eggs, a little at a time,
adding a teaspoonful of flour with each
addition of egg, if the mixture shows signs
of curdling.

4. Fold in the flour carefully and, finally,
stir in the milk, apricots and nuts.

5. Put the mixture into the prepared loaf
tin, smoothing the top level.

6. Bake in a preheated oven, 160°C/
325°F/Gas Mark 3, for 1½ hours, or until a
skewer inserted into the centre of the loaf
comes out clean.

7. As soon as the loaf comes out of the
oven, brush the top with the warmed
honey and sprinkle with the extra
chopped apricots. Leave to cool in the tin
for a few minutes, before turning out and
leaving to cool completely.

TIME: Preparation takes about 20 minutes, and cooking takes about 1½ hours.

VARIATION: Substitute any favourite dried fruit and nuts for the fruit
and nuts suggested in this recipe.

GRANARY ROLLS

For a crisp crust brush the rolls with salted water
and sprinkle with cracked wheat before baking.

MAKES 10

350g/12oz granary flour
1 tsp salt
25g/1oz vegetable fat
12g/½ oz fresh yeast or 2 tsps dried yeast
1 tsp brown sugar
225ml/8fl.oz warm water

1. Place the granary flour and salt in a mixing bowl and leave in a warm place.

2. Melt the vegetable fat in a pan and leave to cool.

3. Cream the yeast and sugar together with three-quarters of the warm water.

4. Make a well in the middle of the flour and pour in the yeast mixture.

5. Add the melted fat and mix to a pliable dough, adding the remaining water as necessary.

6. Knead lightly for a minute or two.

7. Cover with a clean tea towel and leave in a warm place until the dough has doubled in size.

8. Knead again for 3-5 minutes and shape into 10 smooth rolls.

9. Place well apart on a floured baking tray, cover and leave in a warm place until the rolls have doubled in size.

10. Bake in the centre of a preheated oven, 220°C/425°F/Gas Mark 7 for 15-20 minutes or until the rolls sound hollow when tapped underneath.

11. Cool on a wire rack.

TIME: Preparation and proving takes 1 hour, cooking takes 15-20 minutes.

FREEZING: The rolls will freeze well for up to 1 month. Allow to thaw for 1 hour at room temperature before use.

QUICK HOME-MADE BREAD

*The molasses in this recipe gives the
bread an attractive appearance.*

MAKES 3 LOAVES

1150ml/2 pints hand hot water
1 tbsp molasses
1 tbsp sunflower oil
1.5kg/3.3lbs 100% wholemeal flour
2 sachets 'Allison's Easy-Bake Yeast'
3 tsps sea salt

---

1. Set the oven to 220°C/425°F/
Gas Mark 7.

2. Oil three 900g/2lbs bread tins and place them on top of a warm cooker.

3. Fill two 570ml/1 pint jugs with the hand hot water.

4. Add the molasses and oil to one of the jugs, mix and set aside.

5. Place the flour, yeast and salt into a large bowl and mix together thoroughly.

6. Gradually pour the water and molasses mixture into the flour, mixing in with your hands.

7. Add the other jug of water bit by bit until the dough is wettish but not sticky. You may have some water left over.

8. Knead the dough about a dozen times.

9. Divide the dough between the three tins and press down firmly.

10. Leave to rise on the top of the cooker for 5-10 minutes or until the dough has risen near to the top of the tins.

11. Bake in the preheated oven for 35-40 minutes.

TIME: Preparation takes 20 minutes, cooking takes 35-40 minutes.

FREEZING: This bread will freeze well.

SAFFRON BABAS

This is a traditional Easter cake. Cooks spoke in whispers when these cakes were cooking since loud noise was believed to damage the delicate texture!

MAKES 2 CAKES

300g/10oz flour
430ml/¾ pint lukewarm milk
75g/3oz dry yeast
180g/6oz sugar
8 egg yolks
4 egg whites
Rind of 1 lemon
3 tbsps brandy
Pinch saffron powder
900g/2lbs plain flour
Pinch salt
180g/6oz melted butter, slightly cooled
100g/4oz sultanas
2 tbsps candied peel

1. First prepare a batter with 2½ cups flour. Combine the milk and yeast and pour into a well in the centre of the flour. Mix with a wooden spoon and cover the bowl.

2. Leave in a warm place for about 1 hour, covered with a cloth or plastic wrap, until it doubles in bulk and the top becomes bubbly.

3. Combine the sugar together with the egg yolks, egg whites, lemon rind, brandy and saffron. Mix with the yeast mixture and add the remaining flour and salt. Knead the dough by hand for about 30 minutes in the bowl or on a very well-floured surface.

4. Place the dough back in the bowl and add the butter, raisins and peel. Knead the dough by hand until it is smooth and elastic and does not stick. Divide in two equal portions. Butter two 10-inch round cake tins very thickly and place in the dough, patting out evenly. Cover with lightly-oiled plastic wrap and put in a warm place to rise until it fills the pan. Bake in a preheated 200°C/400°F/Gas Mark 6 oven for about 60 minutes.

5. Test with a metal skewer. If the skewer comes out clean when inserted into the centre of the babas the cakes are done. Leave to cool in the pans for about 10-14 minutes and then remove to a cooling rack. Sprinkle with sugar or drizzle with icing.

TIME: Preparation takes about 2 hours, cooking takes about 1 hour.

WATCHPOINT: Do not mix the yeast with milk that is too hot. This can kill the yeast and the cakes will not rise as they should.

POPPY SEED CAKE

This is the Christmas version of an ever popular Polish cake.
As a symbol of holiday generosity, more poppy seeds were
used than in the everyday recipe.

MAKES 2 ROLLS

Pastry Dough
675g/1½ lbs flour
180g/6oz sugar
180g/6oz butter or margarine
2 eggs
90-120ml/3-4fl oz milk
3 tbsps yeast
Pinch salt

Filling
225g/8oz poppy seeds
430ml/¾ pint milk
75g/3oz butter or margarine
140ml/¼ pint honey
4 tbsps ground walnuts
75g/3oz raisins
2 tbsps finely chopped candied peel
2 eggs
100g/4oz sugar
90ml/3fl oz brandy

1. To prepare the dough, cream the butter with the sugar until light and fluffy and gradually add the eggs, beating well in between each addition. Add a pinch of salt and heat the milk until lukewarm. Dissolve the yeast in the milk and add to the other ingredients. Sift in the flour and knead the dough until smooth and elastic.

2. When kneading dough, be sure to stretch it well and work on a lightly-floured surface. If necessary, flour hands if the dough tends to stick. To test if the dough has been sufficiently kneaded, press lightly with two fingers. If the dough springs back fairly quickly, it is ready to leave to rise.

3. Place the dough in a lightly greased bowl, cover with a cloth of lightly greased plastic wrap and leave for about 1 hour, or until doubled in bulk. Keep in a warm place.

4. Bring the milk for the filling to the boil and mix with the poppy seeds. Cook over low heat for about 30 minutes, stirring frequently. Drain the poppy seeds well and blend to a paste in a food processor.

5. Melt the butter and add the honey, walnuts, raisins and peel. Add the poppy seeds and cook for about 15 minutes, stirring frequently over moderate heat.

6. Beat the eggs with the sugar until light and fluffy and combine with the poppy seed mixture. Cook over gentle heat, stirring constantly to thicken. Add the brandy and set the filling aside.

7. When the dough has doubled in bulk, knock it back and knead for a further 2-5 minutes. Divide dough in half. Roll each half out thinly on a floured surface, shaping into rectangles. Spread the filling evenly over each piece and roll up as for a jelly roll. Roll up tightly, pressing the ends together to seal. Place on a lightly buttered baking sheet and curve into a horse shoe shape. Bake in a preheated 190°C/375°F/Gas Mark 5 oven for 45-50 minutes, or until golden brown.

TIME: Preparation takes about 1 hour, cooking takes about 45-50 minutes.

VARIATION: 1 tsp almond or vanilla extract may be used instead of the brandy.

APPLE, PEAR OR PLUM CAKE

Cakes don't always have to be iced sponge layers.
This is made like a flan, using a very versatile biscuit-like pastry.

MAKES 1 CAKE

Pastry
180g/6oz self-raising flour
Salt
3 tbsps sugar
Dash vanilla essence or 1 tsp grated
 lemon rind
150g/5oz butter or margarine
2 egg yolks or 1 whole egg
1-2 tbsps milk or water
Filling
450g/1lb dessert apples, pears or plums
Sugar for dredging

1. Sift the flour with the salt and sugar into a large bowl. Rub in the butter or margarine until the mixture resembles fine breadcrumbs.

2. Make a well in the centre and place in the egg yolks or the whole egg. Add the vanilla or lemon rind and 1 tbsp milk or water. Mix into the flour with a fork. If the pastry appears too dry, add the additional milk or water.

3. Knead together quickly to smooth out.

If the mixture is too soft, wrap well and chill briefly.

4. Press the pastry on the base and up the sides of a flan dish, preferably one with a removable base. Chill for 15 minutes.

5. Meanwhile, prepare the fruit. Peel, core and quarter the apples and slice thinly. Peel, core and quarter the pears and slice those thinly, lengthways. Cut the plums in half and remove the stones. Slice thinly.

6. Arrange the chosen fruit on the base of the flan in straight lines or circles with the slices slightly overlapping. Sprinkle on sugar and bake in a preheated oven at 200°C/400°F/Gas Mark 6 until the pastry is pale golden brown and the fruit is soft. Allow to cool and sprinkle with additional sugar before serving.

TIME: Preparation takes about 30 minutes, cooking takes about 35-40 minutes.

COOK'S TIP: If the pastry begins to brown around the edges before the remaining pastry and fruit is cooked, cover the browned parts with foil, shiny side out.

SERVING IDEAS: Serve with whipped cream, ice cream or pouring cream.
Custard sauce is also a nice accompaniment.

ALMOND TART

This delicious tart can be served as a tea time treat,
or as a dessert with cream.

SERVES 8-10

180g/6oz frozen puff pastry
100g/4oz butter or margarine
100g/4oz caster sugar
2 eggs
100g/4oz self-raising flour
½ tsp almond essence
1 egg-cup of milk
Damson jam
50g/2oz grated almond paste (left
    uncovered in the refrigerator to harden
    before grating)

1. Take ⅔ of the puff pastry, roll it out thinly and line a greased 25cm/10-inch tart plate with it, allowing a 1-inch (2.5cm) overlap all round. Roll out the remainder of the pastry slightly thicker, cut into strips ½ -inch wide and set aside.

2. Cream the slightly softened butter or margarine and sugar together. Add eggs one at a time, beating well. Before adding the second egg, beat in 1 tbsp of the sifted flour.

3. Mix the almond essence with the milk, add to the mixture then fold in the remainder of the flour.

4. Spread the jam on the pastry case to within 1 inch of the rim. Sprinkle the grated almond paste on top. Cover with the sponge mixture using a spatula and taking care to not disturb the filling.

5. Make a lattice with the pastry strips over the top and crimp the edges, turning in the overlap of pastry to form a rim.

6. Bake in the oven at 200°C/400°F/Gas Mark 6 for 20 minutes, then 180°C/350°F/ Gas Mark 4 for a further 15 minutes.

TIME: Preparation takes 25 minutes and cooking takes 35 minutes.

RHUBARB TART

An ideal dessert to make when rhubarb is plentiful.
The juice which is left over makes a refreshing drink
when diluted with chilled soda water.

SERVES 8

900g/2lbs rhubarb, cut into 2.5cm/1 inch
   pieces
525g/1lb 3oz caster sugar
100g/4oz butter
3 eggs
2 tbsps white wine
250g/9oz plain flour
2 tsps baking powder
140ml/¼ pint soured cream
1 tsp ground cinnamon
60g/2oz ground almonds
Icing sugar, to dredge

1. Put the rhubarb into a bowl and sprinkle with 400g/14oz of the sugar. Cover and allow to stand for 1-2 hours.

2. Cream the butter with 90g/3oz of the remaining sugar, until it is light and fluffy.

3. Beat one of the eggs and add this and the wine to the creamed butter and sugar. Sift in the flour and baking powder and mix together well.

4. Knead the base mixture together until it forms a smooth dough. Wrap the dough in greaseproof paper and chill for 30 minutes in the refrigerator.

5. Roll out the dough on a lightly floured board and use it to line a well-greased, loose-based, or spring-clip, 25cm/10 inch round flan tin, pressing the pastry well into the base and up the sides of the tin.

6. Strain the rhubarb and arrange the pieces in the pastry case. Bake in a preheated oven, 180°C/350°F/Gas Mark 4, for 30 minutes.

7. Beat together the cream and the remaining eggs and sugar. Stir in the cinnamon and ground almonds, mixing well to ensure they are thoroughly blended.

8. Remove the flan from the oven and pour the cream topping over the rhubarb. Return the flan to the oven and cook at the same temperature for a further 20-25 minutes, or until the topping is golden brown.

9. Ease the flan out of the tin and cool completely before dredging with icing sugar and serving.

TIME: Preparation takes about 30 minutes, plus 1-2 hours standing time for the rhubarb. Cooking takes 30 minutes for the base, followed by 20-25 minutes for the topping.

VARIATION: Use 900g/2lbs stoned and quartered red plums instead of the rhubarb.

SERVING IDEAS: Serve with whipped double cream.

Index